The Holocaust Museum

by Brenda Haugen

WILSON IMC
OWATONNA, MN

Content Adviser: Harold Marcuse, Ph.D.,
Department of History,
University of California, Santa Barbara

Reading Adviser: Alexa Sandmann, Ph.D.,
Associate Professor of Literacy,
Kent State University

Compass Point Books ✦ Minneapolis, Minnesota

Compass Point Books
3109 West 50th Street, #115
Minneapolis, MN 55410

Visit Compass Point Books on the Internet at *www.compasspointbooks.com*
or e-mail your request to *custserv@compasspointbooks.com*

On the cover: A young woman looks at haunting family photographs in the Tower of Faces, a display at the United States Holocaust Memorial Museum in Washington, D.C.

Photographs: Chuck Pefley/Alamy, cover; Prints Old & Rare, back cover (far left); Library of Congress, back cover, 10; AP Photo, 5, 11, 18, 25; Cynthia Johnson/Time Life Pictures/Getty Images, 6; Bettmann/Corbis, 8, 17, 30; Anthony Potter Collection/Getty Images, 13; Keystone/Getty Images, 14; Mary Evans Picture Library/ Alamy, 15; Imagno/Getty Images, 20; Brendan Smialowski/Getty Images, 22; David Sutherland/Corbis, 23; Ira Nowinski/Corbis, 26; DVIC/NARA, 28; Mario Ruiz/Time Life Pictures/Getty Images, 32; vario images GmbH & Co.KG/Alamy, 35; Tim Sloan/AFP/Getty Images, 36; Brooks Kraft/Corbis, 37; Cameron Davidson/ Alamy, 39; AP Photo/Nick Wass, 40.

Editor: Julie Gassman
Page Production: Ashlee Schultz
Photo Researcher: Eric Gohl
Cartographer: XNR Productions, Inc.
Library Consultant: Kathleen Baxter

Art Director: Jaime Martens
Creative Director: Keith Griffin
Editorial Director: Nick Healy
Managing Editor: Catherine Neitge

Library of Congress Cataloging-in-Publication Data
Haugen, Brenda.
  The Holocaust Museum / by Brenda Haugen.
    p. cm.—(We the people)
Includes bibliographical references and index.
   ISBN-13: 978-0-7565-3357-1 (library binding)
   ISBN-10: 0-7565-3357-0 (library binding)
1. United States Holocaust Memorial Museum—Juvenile literature. 2. Holocaust, Jewish (1939–1945)—Museums—Washington (D.C.)—Juvenile literature. 3. Holocaust, Jewish (1939–1945)—Juvenile literature. 4. Washington (D.C.)—Buildings, structures, etc.—Juvenile literature. I. Title. II. Series.
  D804.175.W18S66 2008
  940.53'18074753—dc22   2007003942

This book was manufactured with paper containing at least 10 percent post-consumer waste.

TABLE OF CONTENTS

We Remember 4

What Was the Holocaust? 8

Creating the Camps 18

At the War's End 26

A Fitting Memorial 30

Never Forgotten 37

Glossary 42

Did You Know? 43

Important Dates 44

Important People 45

Want to Know More? 46

Index 48

WE REMEMBER

Though April 22, 1993, was a gray, miserable spring day, thousands of guests huddled against the cold to be part of a historic event. They would have gladly endured greater discomfort for the right to be at that place at that time. The occasion was the dedication of the United States Holocaust Memorial Museum. The onlookers were there to honor both those who had died and those who had survived.

The opening ceremony featured several honored guests and world leaders, including Bill Clinton, president of the United States. In his speech, Clinton reminded onlookers that "this museum is not for the dead alone, nor even for the survivors who have been so beautifully represented; it is perhaps most of all for those of us who were not there at all. To learn the lessons, to deepen our memories and our humanity."

The speeches ended, and the crowd stepped through the doors and into the past. For Holocaust survivors in

Bud Meyerhoff, chairman of the U.S. Holocaust Council, President Bill Clinton, and Elie Wiesel, founding chairman of the council, lit an eternal flame at the dedication.

attendance, it was a step back into a time of fear, loss, and despair. For those with no personal experience of the Holocaust, it was a step into one of the most brutal periods in human history.

Visitors filed past piles of everyday items that were part of the exhibit: toothbrushes, hairbrushes, umbrellas,

WE ARE THE SHOES, WE ARE THE LAST WITNESSES.
WE ARE SHOES FROM GRANDCHILDREN AND GRANDFATHERS,
FROM PRAGUE, PARIS, AND AMSTERDAM,
AND BECAUSE WE ARE ONLY MADE OF FABRIC AND LEATHER
AND NOT OF BLOOD AND FLESH, EACH ONE OF US AVOIDED THE HELLFIRE.

MOSES SCHULSTEIN (1911–1981),
YIDDISH POET

Visitors to the museum often identify the pile of shoes as one of the most memorable displays.

6

and shoes. These seemingly ordinary items held importance because of what they represented and the victims they once belonged to. Toothbrushes told of countless lost grandmothers and grandfathers. Hairbrushes brought back memories of women tidying their hair. Did the umbrellas belong to men worried about bad weather? Shoes were the most telling. There were workmen's boots, women's pumps, bankers' oxfords, and children's dress shoes. Some had worn soles or broken heels. Each pair represented another person on the long list of Holocaust victims.

For the guests that dreary day, the museum brought forth powerful emotions. Some gasped at what they saw. Others shed tears. Some moved through the many rooms in silence. Everyone understood the museum's main goal: "For the dead and the living, we must bear witness."

WHAT WAS THE HOLOCAUST?

World War I (1914–1918) pitted Germany, Austria-Hungary, and their allies against France, Russia, Great Britain, the United States, and their allies. When Germany was defeated, the country faced serious problems. War debts had mounted, and Germany could not pay what it owed. The country's economy collapsed, and its money became almost worthless. The German people looked for someone to blame for their problems. They also looked for someone to save them.

Members of the National Socialist

In the early 1920s, German money was almost worthless. It was less expensive to use it to start the morning fire than to buy kindling wood.

8

Party, called Nazis, wanted to renew German pride by focusing on ethnic background. A true German, they believed, was an Aryan—a pure-blooded German with blond hair and blue eyes. Nazis felt that only people whom they considered pure Aryans should be allowed in Germany. People of other backgrounds, mainly Jews, were considered racially inferior, or lesser people. They were blamed for the problems Germany faced. Many Germans agreed with the Nazis and believed that Nazi leader Adolf Hitler was their savior.

Within Germany were many diverse groups: Catholics, Lutherans, Jews, Jehovah's Witnesses, and others. The Christian groups were in the majority. Among the minority groups were the Jews. The Nazi party believed that if it got rid of all Jews in Germany, the country would gain power and respect. The Nazi plan for ridding Germany of Jews was called the Final Solution. Years later it would be called the Holocaust.

About 6 million Jews were murdered during the

Holocaust, but they were not the only victims. Another 5 million people—Poles, Gypsies, political prisoners, and people the German government deemed undesirable—were also killed. Some victims were murdered with poison gas, some with bullet wounds, and others with starvation.

Adolf Hitler (1889–1945)

The Holocaust did not happen overnight. It began with the rise to power of Adolf Hitler and continued gradually. When Hitler became the new chancellor, or leader, of the German government in 1933, he gave Germans hope for a better future.

Hitler quickly made changes that gave him more power. He convinced Germans that their country needed him to take greater control if they were to find their way out of poverty and misery. They were willing to give Hitler a chance to turn the country around. Other German leaders kept silent when he took control of the press and political meetings.

As Hitler's powers grew, so did the Nazi party. Within three months of becoming the nation's leader, Hitler had complete rule of the government. He held the full powers

Germans of all ages gave the Nazi salute as the political movement continued to grow in popularity.

of a dictator. He built up a secret police force, called the Gestapo, that spied on ordinary citizens. He ordered camps built as prisons for anyone who opposed his government. He prepared to make his dream of a pure Aryan society a reality.

On April 1, 1933, Hitler's government announced a boycott of Jewish businesses. Days later, the German government passed the first in a series of laws designed to limit the ability of Jews to live and work in Germany. Jews could no longer own land or be newspaper editors. They could not get national health insurance or serve in the military.

At the same time, Hitler sought to persecute other people he labeled as undesirable. On November 24, 1933, the Law Against Habitual and Dangerous Criminals allowed beggars, unemployed workers, alcoholics, homeless people, and political enemies to be sent to concentration camps. It served as another step toward ridding Germany of those considered non-Aryans.

By 1938, Jewish doctors could not see non-Jewish patients, nor could Jews work as accountants or dentists.

A sign on a Jewish store display window in Berlin read, "Germans! Defend yourselves! Don't buy from Jews!"

Jews had to register with the government, listing their property, goods, and money. Jews older than 15 had to carry identity cards.

Many Jewish Poles lived in Germany but had not become citizens. The Nazis wanted Germany for Germans only. In September 1938, 17,000 Jewish Poles were forced to leave Germany. In October, police sent Jews to the Polish border on trains. The Polish government refused to let them enter the country. The nation was not prepared to

Thousands of Jews were stranded near Zbonszyn, Poland, on the German border.

take in such large numbers of people. With nowhere to go, the Jews ended up staying in tent camps in the cold border region between Poland and Germany.

Among those being expelled were the parents of Herschel Grynszpan. At the time, Grynszpan was living in Paris, France. To express his outrage and frustration at the German government over the treatment of his parents, Grynszpan shot and killed an official in Germany's embassy in Paris.

As payback for this murder, Hitler's advisers sent gangs into the streets to attack Jews. They destroyed Jewish homes, businesses, and synagogues throughout Germany. This event, called Kristallnacht, or "Night of Broken Glass," resulted in the looting and destruction of thousands of Jewish businesses and homes. Mobs of Nazis roamed the streets attacking Jews. About 100 Jews died from being beaten. Around 30,000 Jewish

Hundreds of synagogues were destroyed during Kristallnacht. Afterward the Nazis forced Germany's Jewish communities to pay for the cleanup.

15

males were arrested and sent to concentration camps.

Then on September 1, 1939, the German army invaded Poland. The leaders of Great Britain and France had warned Hitler that they would come to Poland's aid if he attacked this neighboring nation. They remained true to their words. Europe erupted into World War II when Britain, France, and other countries tried to help the Poles.

Inside Poland, the German army forced Jewish Poles to move from their homes to ghettos in cities such as Warsaw and Lodz. These ghettos were surrounded by barbed wire, brick walls, and armed guards. They served to confine the country's Jews. In his diary, young Werner Galnick described living in the ghetto: "We had one room—filthy, and the kitchen was also—filthy. … We cleaned the two rooms and lived there. … The SS [Nazi guards] often beat or shot anyone who brought bread, butter, or other food home from work. If it was discovered, the person was either shot, placed in confinement, or punished with blows."

To distinguish them from other Poles, the Nazis

The Nazis built walls, sometimes directly across trolley tracks, to regulate the coming and going of Jews in the ghetto.

required Jewish Poles to wear yellow stars on their clothes. The Jews were required to work all day at hard labor, and then they returned to the walled ghetto, to little food and a life of fear.

These Jewish Poles lost everything: jobs, schools, property, land, and money. In other German-governed areas, Jews led restricted lives with few options.

Those oppressed by the Nazis thought their lives could not get worse. If they could only endure, their problems would end. They had never heard of places like Auschwitz, Buchenwald, Dachau, or Bergen-Belsen.

CREATING THE CAMPS

As World War II spread throughout Europe and Asia, Germany needed people to build roads and work in factories. The cost of providing the military with airplanes, tanks, weapons, and bullets was great. Most German male workers left their jobs to join the military, leaving factories

Prisoners in Dachau produced rifles for the German army.

18

short of workers. Germany needed a tremendous amount of work done cheaply. So the Nazis determined that slave labor was needed. People in some concentration camps became slaves for the Nazis.

By the early 1940s, the Germans ran 5,000 concentration camps, including hundreds of small subcamps. The most infamous camps in Poland were Auschwitz/Birkenau, Majdanek, Sobibor, and Treblinka. The German camps included Buchenwald, Bergen-Belsen, Dachau, and Sachsenhausen. Other camps were opened throughout Europe. At first, in the 1930s, mainly political opponents were sent to the camps. Then Jews, so-called undesirables, Poles, and a host of other groups were imprisoned. It became dangerous to protest when the Gestapo took a man, woman, or family. People feared angering the Nazis and being sent to camps themselves.

When the Nazis decided to empty a ghetto in Poland or another occupied country, police collected people from the area and herded them into railroad cars. The freight

Prisoners were treated like animals and transported in cattle train cars.

cars had no seats, no water or food, no bathrooms, and no heat. People brought suitcases of belongings, which were promptly taken away by the guards. After arriving at the camps, young children and the sick or elderly were taken away to be killed immediately. They could not work, and the Nazis were only interested in labor, not in feeding or caring for others.

At the camps, the people were unloaded like cattle. All personal property was taken and sent to Germany to support the war effort. Camp inmates had their hair shaved and their bodies washed and sprayed for lice. They had to wear striped outfits made of heavy, coarse cotton. Women and girls lived in one set of barracks, men and boys in another. Meals consisted of dry bread and watery soup—a diet of slow starvation. Fences and guards made escape nearly impossible, and the consequences of failing to escape were horrible. Any prisoner caught trying was shot, along with anyone caught helping the escapee.

In Auschwitz, the largest camp, conditions were so bad that often several hundred inmates died in one day. In many camps, deaths were caused by malnutrition, starvation, shootings, beatings, and disease. Inmates in Auschwitz were systematically murdered.

The inmates in Auschwitz also received tattooed identification numbers on their left arms. The tattoos allowed the Nazis to keep an accurate record of the camp victims. It also dehumanized these victims, making them feel like branded animals. The prisoners would be marked forever.

In 1941, Hitler began focusing on the mass murder

A photo display in the Holocaust Museum features the identification tattoos of Auschwitz prisoners.

of Jews. Heinrich Himmler, head of the Nazi SS, visited Auschwitz with new orders: "The Fuhrer [leader] has ordered the Final Solution of the Jewish question. We, the SS, have to carry out this order. ... I ... have chosen Auschwitz for this purpose."

This Final Solution was a programmed extermination of Jews and other undesirables in gas chambers. Specific extermination camps, such as Birkenau, Belzec, and Sobibor, were built to handle the process. Gas chambers were built where hundreds of victims could be killed at one time with poison gas. Ovens to burn the corpses were built near the gas chambers. Their foul-smelling smoke colored the sky.

Author Elie Wiesel, who was taken to Auschwitz with his family in 1944 when he was 15, described seeing the smoke-filled skies over Auschwitz: "Never shall I forget that night, the first night in camp. … Never shall I forget

Today one of the gas chambers at Auschwitz serves as a shrine to its victims.

that smoke. Never shall I forget the little faces of the children, whose bodies I saw turned into wreaths of smoke beneath a silent blue sky." Wiesel's mother and younger sister would be among those who died at Auschwitz.

Birkenau, part of Auschwitz, had four gas chambers that killed up to 8,000 people a day. The ovens designed to cremate the remains could not keep up the pace. Many bodies were buried in trenches that served as mass graves.

Beginning in 1941, guards in some places ordered Jewish prisoners to line up in front of open trenches. The prisoners were machine-gunned, their bodies falling into the mass graves. In 1942, *The New York Times* reported 100,000 Jews from Latvia, Lithuania, and Estonia were murdered in this manner, as well as 100,000 in Poland and possibly 200,000 in the part of Russia that was occupied by Germany.

The Nazis kept records of the number of victims sent to the camps. At Belzec, about 600,000 Jews were murdered. When the camp was no longer useful, the Nazis destroyed it, plowed under the remains, and planted trees to

After liberation, British soldiers discovered a body-filled pit at the Bergen-Belsen concentration camp.

hide the evidence of their crimes.

One year after the extermination camps began, 1 million Jewish men, women, and children had been murdered. But the death rate was too low to satisfy the Nazis, and more death chambers were built. To add to the horror, the people forced to pour the concrete and lay the bricks were later murdered in the gas chambers they had built.

25

AT THE WAR'S END

As the end of the war approached, the Nazis tried to erase all signs of their murderous activities. They hid some camps under lush landscaping. They took apart gas chambers. They dug up mass graves and burned the corpses. But they could not erase all records of what they had done. Tens of

Nazi officials tried to escape punishment for their war crimes by destroying many of the buildings at concentration camps.

thousands of prisoners in occupied countries were sent to Germany in what the prisoners would eventually call death marches. As the Allies advanced, they were shocked at what they found.

The Russian army liberated the first concentration camp, Majdanek, in Poland, in July 1944. From the west, American and British troops arrived in Germany to find horrors beyond their worst nightmares. Extreme starvation was evident in the survivors—men and women who were barely more than living skeletons. Soldiers saw faces that were little more than skin stretched over bone. The filth and smell were overwhelming. U.S. General Dwight D. Eisenhower wrote to leaders in Washington, D.C., "The things I saw beggar description. … The visual evidence and the verbal testimony of starvation, cruelty, bestiality were … overpowering."

The health of the survivors was delicate. They had gone so long without food that they could not digest normal meals. Some died from eating too much too soon. Their

27

In addition to malnutrition, prisoners faced illnesses, such as typhus and dysentery.

bodies simply could not handle food. Others were so near
death that, even though liberated, they did not survive. Said
Leonard Berney, who was with the British troops that freed
Bergen-Belsen, "Many hundreds, perhaps thousands, of
starving people died BECAUSE we fed them the only food

28

we had, our army rations—who in the circumstances could be level-headed enough to think that out in advance?"

World War II in Europe ended on May 8, 1945, after the formal surrender by the Germans. Eleven million people had been killed as part of the Nazi effort to rid the world of Jews, Poles, Slavs, Gypsies, socialists, and anyone else who did not fit the Nazi plan. Roughly two-thirds of all Jews living in Europe were killed in the Holocaust. Those who survived were left homeless, penniless, hungry, and sick. The effects of the Nazis' Final Solution reached across Europe and lasted for decades.

A FITTING MEMORIAL

More than 30 years passed before the United States began work on a memorial to the millions lost in the Holocaust. In 1978, President Jimmy Carter formed a council on the Holocaust, with Elie Wiesel as chairman. The council recommended three actions. First, a memorial should be

On September 27, 1979, Chairman Elie Wiesel (right) spoke about the Holocaust and provided President Carter with the council's recommendations.

30

erected to those who were lost and those who survived. Second, an education center needed to be set up for those who wished to learn about the Holocaust. Finally, the United States should establish a national Day of Remembrance to honor the dead.

The U.S. government donated nearly 2 acres (0.8 hectares) of land near the National Mall in Washington, D.C., as the site for the museum. Money for the actual building came from private donations. In all, the museum would cost $168 million: $90 million for the building and $78 million for the exhibits. James Ingo Freed, whose family fled Nazi Germany when he was 9 years old, was chosen to be the project architect.

Before starting his design, Freed visited sites of concentration camps in Europe. His design combined three elements of Holocaust culture: the *shtetls* (Jewish villages in eastern Europe), the architecture of concentration camps, and the walls of ghettos where Jews in places such as Warsaw and Lodz had been forced to live. Freed's goal was

The museum, designed by James Ingo Freed, won the American Institute of Architecture Honor Award in 1994.

"to make a building that allows for horror, sadness. I don't know if you can make a building that does this, if you can make an architecture of sensibility."

Freed planned for the permanent exhibit to take up three floors. There would be space for an education and research center and for temporary exhibits. A Hall of Remembrance would provide visitors with a quiet place for reflection.

On October 16, 1985, soil and ashes from many concentration camps were buried beneath the site where the museum would stand. A year later, 15th Street, the road in front of the museum site, was renamed Raoul Wallenberg Place. Wallenberg, a Swedish diplomat,

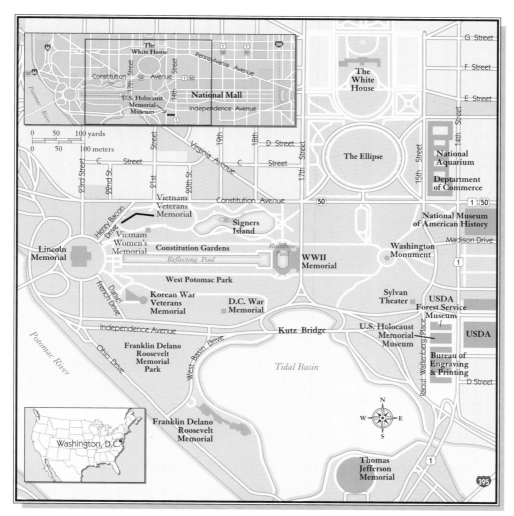

The museum is near the National Mall in Washington, D.C.

saved the lives of thousands of Jews. He provided them
with documents saying they could move to Sweden. In 1988,
President Ronald Reagan attended the setting of the

33

cornerstone, while artifacts began to be collected for exhibits.

In 1993, the dream of a national memorial to the Holocaust finally became a reality. The United States Holocaust Memorial Museum includes 265,000 square feet (23,850 square meters) of exhibit space—the equivalent of almost five football fields. The permanent exhibit forms the focal point of the museum. It presents documents, artifacts, and photos that explain what occurred during the Holocaust and how it came about. The exhibit is divided into three main parts, each on its own floor: the Nazi Assault, the Final Solution, and the Last Chapter. Audio and video histories give visitors a glimpse into the Holocaust.

On the lower level, the Children's Tile Wall serves as a remembrance of the 1.5 million children killed during the Holocaust. To build this wall, American children drew their ideas about the Holocaust on small tiles. More than 3,000 tiles were placed in the wall as part of the permanent memorial.

Each year special exhibits are presented at the museum.

The Tower of Faces is a three-story area covered with photos from a small village in present-day Lithuania. All but 29 of the villagers were killed in the Holocaust.

One exhibit was about Anne Frank, a Jewish girl in Amsterdam, the Netherlands, who hid in an attic for several years to avoid being discovered by the Nazis. After World War II ended, Anne's diary was found, telling the story of her years in hiding. Another powerful exhibit focused on other hidden children. Friends and strangers alike risked their lives to protect individual Jews and hid

35

Many visitors are overwhelmed with sadness after experiencing the museum.

them from the Nazis. Many of those children lived in basements or closets to avoid being captured or killed.

In its first 14 years, more than 24 million people visited the museum and learned about the suffering of the Holocaust victims. Nearly 8 million of those guests were schoolchildren. More than 17 million visitors were non-Jews.

NEVER FORGOTTEN

The United States Holocaust Memorial Museum serves as a constant reminder that the horrors of the past must never be repeated. To fulfill that goal, the museum provides education and an outreach program to carry its message beyond the museum walls.

The museum records survivors' stories, oral histories by the people who lived through the Holocaust. These stories tell of people hiding in shacks, basements, and trenches to avoid capture. They are the tales of children who lost homes, families, and friends. Bart Stern, born in Hungary in 1926,

The museum honors survivors by collecting and displaying basic survivor information and providing contacts between survivors.

37

explained, "It was by the greatest miracle that I survived. …
I was hiding out in the heap of dead bodies because in the
last week … the crematoria didn't function at all." Charlene
Schiff from Poland described how she lived in the forests:
"I ate worms. I ate bugs. I ate anything that I could put in
my mouth."

Traveling exhibitions help bring the story of the
Holocaust to other places beyond the walls of the museum.
About 1 million people have attended these presentations.
"Remember the Children: Daniel's Story" is a particu-
larly moving exhibit. "Daniel's Story" is a history of the
Holocaust specifically designed for children ages 8 and
older. This exhibit shows how life changed for one Jewish
family when the Nazis gained control of Germany. The
story is told through the eyes of Daniel, who was 11 when
the Nazis came to power.

Education is a primary function of the museum. Special
programs for teachers explain how to address Holocaust top-
ics in the classroom. The museum helps educate future U.S.

military officers and current law enforcement officers about their roles in preserving democracy. Special classes educate Catholic schoolteachers on the Catholic Church's role during the Holocaust. A literacy program about Holocaust history rounds out the museum's educational opportunities.

In addition to exhibits, the museum is home to a research library, two theaters, a computer center, classrooms, a memorial space, and areas for discussion.

39

It is not enough for the museum to serve as a reminder of the horrors of genocide in the past. Conferences and programs sponsored by the museum work to stop mass murder of any people in any place. In 2004, concern for the people of Darfur in Sudan, Africa, attracted the museum's efforts to bring awareness of the genocide there.

Not everyone can travel to Washington, D.C., to visit

In 2006, photographs of scenes in Darfur and Chad were projected onto the museum's exterior walls, bringing attention to the tragedies taking place in the African nations.

the Holocaust Museum, but they can visit the museum online. The museum's Web site offers many of the same materials available to those who visit in person. Texts, photographs, and videos can be accessed on the Web site.

The United States Holocaust Memorial Museum offers a profound and moving learning experience. It is peaceful and quiet. It is honest. At the museum's dedication, President Clinton said, "The Holocaust reminds us for- ever that knowledge divorced from values can only serve to deepen the human nightmare; that a head without a heart is not humanity."

The Holocaust Museum helps people remember, with the hope that individuals will be inspired to work together to protect the rights of all people wherever they live.

GLOSSARY

Aryan—a term used by Nazis to describe a supposed master race of pure-blooded Germans with blond hair and blue eyes

concentration camps—prison camps where thousands of inmates are held under harsh conditions

dictator—a ruler who takes complete control of a country, often unjustly

extermination—killing or destroying someone or something

genocide—the organized killing of a large number of people

ghettos—areas in European towns where the Jewish population was forced to live

liberated—freed from someone or some group

malnutrition—a lack of healthy foods in the diet

Nazis—members of the National Socialist Party that came to power in Germany under the leadership of Adolf Hitler in 1933

persecute—to continually treat in a cruel and unfair way

Poles—natives of Poland or people of Polish descent

DID YOU KNOW?

- The United States has nearly 60 Holocaust museums in cities throughout the country.

- More than 70 videos in the permanent collection tell the story of the Holocaust to museum visitors.

- The museum houses more than 12,000 artifacts and pieces of artwork and 37 million pages of historical documents.

- The museum's survivors' registry lists 194,915 survivors and their families from 59 countries.

- More than 8,700 oral history videotapes preserve the personal stories of what happened during the Holocaust.

- In the museum, visitors walk through an actual boxcar that carried prisoners to concentration camps. Replicas of paving stones from the Warsaw ghetto make up part of the museum floor.

- As recommended by the U.S. Holocaust Memorial Council, the United States honors victims each spring on the Day of Remembrance. The date changes every year but is always in April. In many countries, January 27, the day Auschwitz was liberated, is celebrated as Holocaust memorial day.

IMPORTANT DATES

Timeline

1933	Adolf Hitler is appointed chancellor of Germany, and the first concentration camp, Dachau, is opened.
1938	Kristallnacht, the "Night of Broken Glass," finds rioters terrorizing Jews in Austria, Germany, and other Nazi-controlled areas.
1939	On September 1, Germany invades Poland.
1943	The Final Solution becomes more urgent to the Nazis, and a mass extermination of Jews is undertaken; Auschwitz is chosen as the major extermination camp site.
1944	Soviet troops liberate the concentration camp at Majdanek.
1945	World War II ends.
1978	President Jimmy Carter asks a committee to plan a fitting Holocaust memorial in the United States.
1985	Ground is broken for building the United States Holocaust Memorial Museum.
1993	A dedication ceremony opens the museum.

IMPORTANT PEOPLE

ANNE FRANK (1929–1945)

A young Jewish girl remembered for her diary, written while hiding from the Nazis during World War II; she hid in the attic of Dutch friends' house in Amsterdam for two years before being sent to a concentration camp, where she died

ADOLF HITLER (1889–1945)

Austrian veteran of World War I who came to be chancellor of Germany; led the German Nazi movement to promote Aryan purity; the Holocaust was part of Hitler's plan to rid Germany of Jews and other people he felt were undesirable

RAOUL WALLENBERG (1912–1947?)

A Swedish diplomat who saved the lives of thousands of European Jews by providing them with papers that said they could move to Sweden; at the end of the war, he was arrested by the Soviets, who thought he might be an American spy; he disappeared without a trace

ELIE WIESEL (1928–)

Holocaust survivor who wrote about his experiences in a famous book called Night; *served as chairman of the U.S. Holocaust Memorial Council and is a professor at Boston University*

WANT TO KNOW MORE?

At the Library

Altman, Linda Jacobs. *Impact of the Holocaust*. Berkeley Heights, N.J.: Enslow
    Publishers, 2004.

Altman, Linda Jacobs. *Simon Wiesenthal*. San Diego: Lucent Publishing, 2000.

Bartoletti, Susan Campbell. *Hitler Youth: Growing Up in Hitler's Shadow*. New York:
    Scholastic, 2005.

Cretzmeyer, Stacy. *Your Name Is Renée: Ruth Kapp Hartz's Story as a Hidden Child in
    Nazi-Occupied France*. New York: Oxford University Press, 1999.

Haugen, Brenda. *Adolf Hitler: Dictator of Nazi Germany*. Minneapolis: Compass
    Point Books, 2006.

Lowry, Lois. *Number the Stars*. New York: Yearling Books, 2005.

Schroeder, Peter W. *Six Million Paper Clips: The Making of a Children's Holocaust
    Memorial*. Minneapolis: Kar-Ben Publishing, 2004.

Warren, Andrea. *Surviving Hitler: A Boy in the Nazi Death Camps*. New York:
    HarperTrophy, 2001.

On the Web

For more information on this topic, use FactHound.

1. Go to *www.facthound.com*

2. Type in this book ID: 0756533570

3. Click on the *Fetch It* button.

FactHound will find the best Web sites for you.

On the Road

**United States Holocaust
Memorial Museum**
100 Raoul Wallenberg Place
Washington, DC 20024-2126
202/488-0400
Exhibits, films, and educational
material on the Holocaust

Houston Holocaust Memorial
5401 Caroline St.
Houston, TX 77004
713/942-8000
Displays that show the progression of
the Holocaust, from the disruption of
normal life to extermination

Look for more We the People books about this era:

The 19th Amendment
The Berlin Airlift
The Civil Rights Act of 1964
The Dust Bowl
Ellis Island
The Great Depression
The Korean War
Navajo Code Talkers
Pearl Harbor

The Persian Gulf War
The San Francisco Earthquake of 1906
September 11
The Sinking of the USS Indianapolis
The Statue of Liberty
The Titanic
The Tuskegee Airmen
The Vietnam Veterans Memorial

A complete list of We the People titles is available on our Web site:
www.compasspointbooks.com

INDEX

Aryans, 9, 12
Auschwitz/Birkenau concentration camp, 17, 19, 21, 22, 23–24
Austria-Hungary, 8

Belzec extermination camp, 22–23, 24–25
Bergen-Belsen concentration camp, 17, 19, 28–29
Birkenau. *See* Auschwitz/Birkenau concentration camp.
boycotts, 12
Buchenwald concentration camp, 17, 19

Carter, Jimmy, 30
Catholic Church, 9, 39
Children's Tile Wall, 34
Clinton, Bill, 4, 41
concentration camps, 12, 16, 17, 19, 20–21, 22–24, 27, 28–29, 31
cost, 31

Dachau concentration camp, 17, 19
Darfur region, 40
Day of Remembrance, 31
death marches, 27
dedication ceremony, 4, 41

education center, 31, 32, 37, 38–39
Eisenhower, Dwight D., 27
exhibits, 5, 7, 31, 32, 34–35, 38
extermination camps, 22–23, 25

factories, 18–19
Final Solution, 9, 22–23, 29
France, 8, 14–15, 16

Frank, Anne, 35
Freed, James Ingo, 31–32

gas chambers, 22–23, 24, 25, 26
Germany, 8–9, 10–12, 13, 14–15, 16, 18, 19, 24, 27, 29
Gestapo, 12, 19
ghettos, 16–17, 19, 31
Great Britain, 8, 16, 27
Grynszpan, Herschel, 14–15
Gypsies, 10, 29

hairbrushes, 5, 7
Hall of Remembrance, 32
Hitler, Adolf, 9, 10–12, 15, 16, 21–22

identification numbers, 21
identity cards, 13

Kristallnacht ("Night of Broken Glass"), 15–16

Law Against Habitual and Dangerous Criminals, 12
liberation, 27
Lodz, Poland, 16, 31

Majdanek concentration camp, 19, 27
mass graves, 24, 26
memorial, 30–31

Nazis, 8–9, 13, 20, 22, 24, 25, 31

ovens, 23, 24

Poland, 13–14, 16, 19, 24, 27

Poles, 10, 13, 16, 17, 19, 29
political prisoners, 10

railroad cars, 19–20
Raoul Wallenberg Place, 32
Reagan, Ronald, 33–34
records, 24, 26
"Remember the Children: Daniel's Story" presentation, 38
Russia, 8, 24, 27

Sachsenhausen concentration camp, 19
shoes, 7
shtetls (Jewish villages), 31
size, 34
slave labor, 19, 20
Sobibor concentration camp, 19, 22–23
starvation, 10, 21, 27–29
survivors, 4–5, 37–38

tattoos, 21
toothbrushes, 5, 7
Treblinka concentration camp, 19

umbrellas, 5, 7
undesirables, 10, 12, 19, 22
United States, 4, 8, 27, 30, 31

visitors, 4–5, 32, 34, 36

Wallenberg, Raoul, 32–33
Warsaw, Poland, 16, 31
Web site, 41
Wiesel, Elie, 23–24, 30
World War I, 8
World War II, 16, 18, 29

About the Author

Brenda Haugen started in the newspaper business and had a career as an award-winning journalist before finding her niche as an author. Since then, she has written and edited many books, most of them for children. A graduate of the University of North Dakota in Grand Forks, Brenda lives in North Dakota with her family.